THE TINKERBELL HILTON DIARIES

THE TINKERBELL HILTON DIARIES

MY LIFE TAILING PARIS HILTON

TINKERBELL HILTON
AS TOLD TO D. RESIN

WARNER BOOKS

New York   Boston

Copyright 2004 by Philip Brooke
All right reserved.

Warner Books

Time Warner Book Group
1271 Avenue of the Americas, New York, NY 10020
Visit our Web site at www.twbookmark.com.

Printed in the United States of America

First Printing: September 2004
10 9 8 7 6 5 4 3 2 1

Library of Congress Control Number: 2004108587
ISBN: 0-446-69430-4

Cover design by Brigid Pearson
Book design and text composition by Mada Design

Author's Note

Lather. Rinse. Repeat.

You know what happens.

You're cruising along in life, enjoying a simple everyday pleasure, say, a good cup of hot coffee from some fast-food place. Then, out of the blue, you have your intelligence completely insulted by some amazing warning label that makes you wonder what the hell kind of planet you live on, where people need to be told stunningly obvious things like "not for use with crotch" or "really, it's amazingly hot, don't try to hold this with your crotch" or even "look, it's just not worth it, your car almost certainly has a cup holder, or at least you could stuff the cup between the parking brake and the seat, but not, for the love of God, on your crotch; I mean c'mon, don't be a hero, it's too hot to drink now anyway, be reasonable."

Warning labels. The real yardstick of society. Not soap, not our jails, not that genome thing that ordinary people pretend to understand but don't. Warning labels. The real thing anthropologists will judge us by, the way you judge ancient people who used to toss perfectly good virgins into perfectly upset volcanos rather than just take their virgins with them and go find a place to live where maybe the volcano is just sort of off in the distance.

Well, I'm here to warn you that you're reading a humorous, exaggerated sort of diary—written by a dog. It's a parody, a satire, a bit of a spoof on what a dog might think and write about. If he could. Though, not yet, since we're being careful, you're actually reading the warning label that leads up to it all.

Anyway, I'm here to tell you once again, in case the cover didn't do it for you, that you're reading fiction.

What you're about to read is not in any way to be construed as a precise factual account. Sure, you're a little disappointed since you thought you'd stumbled across a rich vein of gossip, what with a pet keeping a diary about its life with a celebrity. "Hey, gadzooks, what a find!" you said out loud in the bookstore, startling those around you, but the clubs in this book are made up, the events described after this point are simply not real, there is no *Amenorrhea* magazine, and, as far as I know, the Dalai Lama and Paris have never conversed.

Now that you've been warned, go ahead and read. And enjoy.

FOR MARY MCGUIRE

Acknowledgments

Much thanks to: Satan, The Mighty Katgyrl, John Aherne, Liz Spiers, Choire Sicha, Ana Marie Cox, Maud Newton, Metafilter, The 9622 Monkeys, Kate Lee, my Scotland People, Al Gore for that handy interweb dealy, Madeleine Schachter—and last because she's absolutely first, Mom.

No thanks to: unbelievably white '80s rock group Boston and the neighbors who love them.

PREFACE

YOU KNOW ME.

I'm very easy to spot these days; I'm that freaky little thing in any recent photo of Paris Hilton, clinging to her side against the supernova glow of her publicity.

No, you're picturing younger Hilton sister Nicky . . . I understand your mistake, but that's not me. I'm on the other side, the one that looks like a fuzzy rodent-flavored bouillon cube that you might get a reasonably large rat from if you added enough water to it.

No, no, that's Nicole Richie you're thinking of now.

Look, I'm the dog.

Yes, that's me. Tink Hilton: Fashion Accessory To The Heiress.

Pretty apt term that, *accessory*, since my owner's barely there sense of fashion always makes me feel like I'm involved in some sort of decency crime. If mentally mumbled phrases wore out from use like vinyl records do, by now my personal copy of "man, you're lucky that you're pretty" would have more snaps and pops in it than Barbara Walters's spine when she farts.

But I digress. I'm not here to mock my owner's fashion sense. Well, not on every page.

No, I'm here to tell you about My Paris Hilton Year.

I've kept a journal, see.

You would, too, if you found yourself in my gaudy pink high-label dog booties (I'm guessing they're Louis Vuitton), found yourself held near more celebrity faces than Botox, found yourself passed around more social events than herpes.

I know what you're thinking: many of you reading this might dislike Paris Hilton. You possibly find her plastic, spoiled, vapid, and long ago pampered out of any sense of reality by an amazing fairy-tale-of-a-life. You boggle at how one who essentially does nothing can receive so much press and easy praise for what seems like not much more than just showing up half dressed and fully inconvenienced.

You're not necessarily wrong. But if that's all there was, you wouldn't have read this far. As a cultural phenomenon, just like the old cliché goes, you love her *because* you hate her.

Why?

Damned if I know. I'm a teacup Chihuahua, not a psychologist. I figure people out mostly by how their crotch smells—who knows why you do what you do. I'm still trying to figure out why you all watch Jay Leno.

Nevertheless, worthy or not, a cultural icon Paris unavoidably is, and I should know since I have been physically closer to Paris than anyone else during what has been her most publicized, and likely the most interesting, time in her life: the year between my arrival on Halloween 2002 and the sex-tape incident of November 2003, which irrevocably changed the way much of the world sees her.

It was during this time, probably while you were foolishly wasting time with some sort of menial job or child rearing, when the name *Paris Hilton* suddenly went from the outer periphery of the tabloid universe to a mantra repeated by the celebrity news circuit, not unlike a shark attack victim washed up on a beach, rocking back and forth and gibbering something about a big fish.

This, I point out, all happened while a war was going on.

That's celebrity.

Since I was there for most of it, I have tried to put everything down while it was happening . . . no mean feat when you lack discrete digits or the ability to stop people from just picking you up and stuffing you into a handbag whenever the hell they please. The whole world is my Winona Ryder.

Unfortunately, I then sent all of these carefully collected notes from the field to some barely literate weblogger with a name even goofier than mine to collate and edit into a collected work, which he claims he can get published as a book.

Actually, I sent my stuff to a lot of webloggers—I think that's the real talent pool these days . . . also, none of them have jobs and will say yes to anything—but let me tell you it's not easy to get someone to publish a journal written by a dog—no matter how famous.

All he did was ask me for money, and if I could get him some of the Olsen twins' underwear.

The Internet. It just lets anyone on it, doesn't it.

I'll be very surprised if anyone ever gets to see any of this.

If you do, I hope you enjoy it.

—Tinkerbell Hilton

Nov. 01 | 02

I've been Paris Hilton's dog for just under twenty-four hours now. I've been on both coasts, two airplanes, and three parties that you weren't invited to. Since yesterday. Afternoon.

Paris is like the United States Army of slack . . . Paris Hilton will kill more time by 7 a.m. than most people will, ever.

I'm coming to you now live from a limo somewhere between here and Rodeo Drive, where I've been informed we will "get me looking right" for the film premiere we have scheduled for this evening. Discovering she didn't bring her credit card, Paris has wondered aloud if the five thousand in loose cash she has on her will be enough for "the dog stuff."

I have to say, for an animal that's been so forcefully bred behind the genetic eight ball that taking a shit requires me to stand on my tippy toes, this is shaping up to be quite a life.

Nov. 02 | 02 GRAVY STAIN

I had no idea dog food came in this many varieties.

Up until now I've been living on stuff that I thought was food. It kept me alive and I got it twice a day.

Here, it's *food*. Little bits of meat in gravy.

Plus, I've got the snack thing wired down tight . . . all I have to do is wait by the top of the stairs on the second floor for a servant to bring a tray (they do it every few hours or so) and pop out at the last possible second, lean all my weight to one side like the Duke boys putting the General on two wheels, and bingo, a food storm. The food I can snag off the floor before the servant tries to kill me with whatever hand isn't holding his sprained ankle in place, or applying pressure to staunch a flow of blood is all mine.

I think this is what it's like when you people discover Internet porn for the first time. "I'm never leaving the house, ever!" I said aloud to a Pomeranian.

Three Pomeranian dogs also live here in the LA house, and they're all completely stupid. Pomeranians are the dog equivalent of the short bus kids: you sort of have to be patient with them. Unfortunately, because they're small, yappy, and ubiquitous, they're the ones most people picture when they hear the term "toy dog." Real fond of barking at nothing and getting freaked out by their own tails. Not exactly Lassie. In fact, if they had done that show with a Pomeranian dog, it would have been much simpler: Timmy would fall down the well, Lassie would furiously lick itself for forty minutes, and then Lassie would turn around and psychotically challenge a small rock to a fight, which it would ultimately become intimidated by.

Getting away from the Pomeranians isn't too hard, as not too many moments tick by without Paris fussing over me in some way. It's not bad, it's just . . . I mean, the novelty has to wear off a little eventually, right?

MY NEW OWNER

So far Paris has a slack, blank, almost Zen sort of ease that's like wallpaper to read but seems like it will be pretty easy to get along with.

Yesterday during brunch she knocked a skewerlike fondue fork off the edge of her table, which sailed into her thigh like a dart. It took her a full five minutes to even notice. The fork just sat there as if some tiny Columbus had annexed her left leg for the glory of Spain. I was too stunned to bark. When Paris did happen to glance down, she peeled the paper top off an individual pat of butter, yanked out the slightly impaled fork, and applied the paper as you would a patch on a rubber dingy.

She did all of this slowly, and I never saw any blood. Since she was wearing capri pants, I briefly wondered if her leg was actually fake, but her ankle was clearly flesh. You can't have a fake leg with a real foot, can you?

In any event, that's pretty calm. She makes Miles Davis look like the Tasmanian devil.

Paris's sister Nicky is a little more of what you'd think of as normal, in that you don't find yourself wondering if she has any fake limbs.

NOV 04 | 02 WRONG

Oh, for the love of God. . .

I'm in a pink angora sweater.

Here I thought I was a *pet*, right, a companion, not a hood ornament. Turns out they couldn't get me to a specialty toy dog store on Rodeo Drive fast enough to put me in a pink angora sweater and place a big pink bow on my head.

I'm one of those dogs now . . . the kind that people cheer when a falcon swoops down and disappears into the sky with one in its talons.

We were noble animals once, you know. Chihuahuas were bred to be familiars to royalty. My kind was once thought to serve as a guide for the human soul after death.

I just saw my reflection in the limo window—I look like the shit that a very flamboyant shark would take after it ate Isaac Mizrahi.

I would try to kick my own ass if I met me. Splendid.

Nov 05 | 02
Reach Out and Torch Someone

Keeping up this journal won't be too hard, that's for sure. Paris has some sort of cell phone fetish: one or more of just about every form of tiny personal messaging device ever invented belongs to her arsenal. Handy for thumb-sized paws.

This morning I swiped a phone—messenger roughly the size of John Ashcroft's libido from a pile of about fifteen on Paris's nightstand. She thinks it's adorable that her dog wants to be like her "mommy."

I'll bet Joan Crawford thought the same thing when the kid asked for a typewriter.

Seriously, I'm being made to wear a tiny scarf as I type this. I barely have a neck, mind you, but look, I get to have a scarf.

The scarf has bunnies on it.

ΠOV 06 | 02 WHERE İ'M COMING FROM

I should tell you about myself briefly:

First of all, toy dogs like myself have it rougher than you probably think. Folks pay a lot of lip service to care and love and how special we all are, but the fact is there's a long waiting list of very wealthy potential owners all vying for a select few of us, so right from birth we're raised and constantly groomed by our breeders to be the most profitable fashion accessory that we can be for their very exclusive clientele. If it turns out that you're not cute enough, or cute in the wrong way, you get sent either to the pound or to "visit" some guy in Wyoming who sells novelty taxidermy, like turtles with beaver tails, Jackalopes, toy poodle heads on St. Bernard bodies . . . the sort of thing extremely stoned college students buy for use as ottomans and then sell at tag sales as soon as the bong hits wear off. That's a lot of pressure to be adorable.

Most toy dogs play by the rules and quietly bide their time until they get selected. I figured this for a sucker's game, waiting for some lonely octogenarian with more money than sense to pick up a new surrogate child she can dress funny and parade about like a tiny Gay Pride float with organs. I got proactive. I snuck onto my breeder's laptop after hours and learned how to type. Well, first I figured out how to type on it without sliding off of its surface

like a tick on a Skittle, and then I learned to type. After that it didn't take me too long to figure out the whole e-mail thing, and it was a short jump from that to news groups, where I started floating the idea that teacup Chihuahuas were the hot accessory this season. After a few weeks of that, my breeder, the most prominent in the area, got an e-mail that the Paris Hilton was looking for a teacup Chihuahua. That was pretty much that. I e-mailed Paris back, told her that we had just what she was after, and she should hurry right over.

Hey, you'd move in with her too if you could.

Next thing I know, I'm in the back of yet another limo, named "Tinkerbell," and looking like Christopher Lowell's used angora Q-tip.

Good thinking, me.

Nov. 20 | 02 Homestyle

Paris and Nicole are quite a sight: Nicole is sporting a leopard-print miniskirt, a midriff baring . . . well, I can't prove it, but it looks like a top made from a bunch of those nipples you pump air into a tire from, and a hairstyle that looks like a lion stuck its head in an industrial dryer. She looks like a cross between a hooker and a World War II marine mine.

If the Thunderdome has one of those *American Idol* shows, Nicole is dressed like that particularly wince-inducing losing contestant you can't shake remembering the next morning.

Paris herself is wearing what appears to be a skirt made out of a blue bandana and a skimpy bikini bra made from pink and baby blue bath mats . . . maybe "appears" is the wrong word, I've heard she often makes her own stuff, and I think I saw a pink and blue bath mat in the LA house.

They seem to run pretty fast and loose with the couture, here. Listen, my hide matches suede . . . if she gets bored with me, I don't want to end up as a hat or something. If I suddenly start not showing up in pictures without an explanation, please call the police.

DEEP THOUGHTS

Wisely, we're leaving a ridiculously bad movie right after Paris's cameo flashes past, and we've joined a group of C-list celebs hovering around outside. I don't know who any of these people are, except for the Osbourne kids Kelly and Jack, who it turns out really talk like that in real life.

There are now about eight of us, everyone stuffed into this one limo. The Osbourne kids are the soundtrack for the ride. Listen in for a moment and understand my misery:

Jack: "You know your fingernails keep growing after you die."

Kelly: "No they don't, your hand just shrinks."

Jack: "Shrinks?"

Kelly: "Like shrivels, from the heat of your decomposing flesh."

Jack: "What? Heat? You don't g— Paris, tell her you don't give off heat after you die—"

Kelly: "Aren't farts hot? You give off the same gas, which is all fart, so it's probably hot."

Paris didn't get to respond, as Nicole shut the two of them up by energetically vomiting on their heads, by far the best response anyone could have thought up.

I hope the battery on this phone holds out, because if I have to listen to their inane chatter without something to distract myself, I'm going to nose open the window and take my chances with the LA traffic.

Nov. 21 | 02 10:24 P.M.

Hear that steady pounding thud? We're mobile. By "we," I mean myself, Paris, Nicole, and two guys who are one-half of some boy band. Evidently, the hot look for right now is "ghetto fabulous," and they are indulging in the ghetto look with cornrowed hair and gold caps on their teeth.

Cornrows on white guys. They look like potatoes that Ray Charles peeled in the back of a moving bus. Great move, guys.

We are all in one of those Humvee things, and the two-boy band desperadoes are throwing what they think are gang signs at each other. The Hummer has little decal stickers on the side of it designed to look like bullet holes.

This is deeply uncool. I'd like to tell you that a group of superwealthy Hills kids paying a couple hundred thousand dollars to put out some faux ghetto style is a kind of high-minded statement they're making about not being bullied into being told what to do by the reactionary white liberal guilt segment of California's cognoscenti by knowingly wallowing in a vulgar open mockery of poverty and crime, but I don't think they even know what any of those words mean.

When everyone is appropriately distracted, I'm taking a shit in Paris's handbag.

Paris is dancing along to the beat in the way that paraplegics or Pink might, from only the torso up, with a lot of pointing to stuff that isn't there. The people in the cars going by might think she's having some sort of very calm seizure, because it doesn't particularly match up to the beat.

Nicole is still very unconscious from her earlier drinking from a can of brake fluid, which she managed to get through about half of before realizing what she was doing.

. . . you know, now that I take a look out the window, this isn't the part of town where I thought I overheard we were headed to. And we've been driving far too long. In fact, I think I sort of recognize things a little . . .

Hey, this isn't right. Better say something, they're actually sort of in danger down here.

Hey, genius at the wheel! Quit just following whatever directions the GPS screen tells you, something is wrong. *Hey*. Look out the window. Don't you notice an awful lot of pawn shops going by? Little seedy for Westgate, don't you think? *Hey!*

Great, now the Heiress is scolding me for barking.

Look out the window.

Ugh. The boy band is too busy looking tough to the other drivers to notice; they're just blindly following the GPS screen.

I read once when they shot that monkey into space they gave his capsule a bunch of fake controls so it'd have something to twist when it wanted to feel in control. I'll bet that monkey figured out what was going on faster than these two.

Ugh. May as well relax and wait until someone figures out that we're way, way off. Better do it soon, we're not too far from the roughest—

What . . . oh, here we go, the car is stalling.

Well, we're fully stalled now. In the middle of Compton . . . In a $55,000 screaming yellow zonker–colored Humvee with bullet hole stickers on the outside, two out-of-it models and two photo negatives of Latrell Sprewell look-alikes on the inside.

You know, I take back all of my complaining from before, things are shaping up to be pretty funny.

Fake Sprewell number two is starting to freak out. Maybe he recognizes where we are from his favorite gangsta rap video. To her credit, Paris is as blissed out and calm as ever, but I think that's because she doesn't really get her situation yet. I doubt that she's ever been down here.

Oh hey, look . . . company. That was quick.

Say, maybe this nice fourteen-year-old with the gang colors and huge face tattoo can help. She certainly seems interested. Oh, she doesn't appear to be speaking English. Well, maybe her friend does, the one with the sunglasses on in the middle of the night.

This is great. The two girls outside have their faces pressed up against the glass. I think the sunglasses girl only has one eyeball under there . . . she has a big knife scar going down that side of her face.

Boy Band boy number two is crying. Not merely sniffling, but the sort of deep, deep sobbing you get when you've just given up all pretense of manliness and you just revert back to a prepubescent state. The girl gangs down here are worse than the guys—maybe he only looks dumb.

I think Paris is hip to the situation now. She's trying to get 911 on her cell phone. They might actually show up in this part of town if they really believe that it's Paris on the phone, but then again, they might not.

Now the gang chick with the Queequeg face outside is tapping on the glass and laughing because it makes both of the boys inside jump every time she does it.

God, I wish I could take pictures with this phone.

Nov. 22 | 02 Speaking in Tongues

Paris seems somewhat ADD-affected, which is the polite way people have come to describe what's left of your mind when you watch too much TV as a kid and lose the power to focus on anything longer than the first two instructions on a box of Pop-Tarts. Add to that a willing embrace of air-headed Valley Girl–speak, ten or fifteen Red Bulls, and Nicole in the room, and you get the sort of dialogue William Burroughs would have written if he got tired of being so straightforward and easy to follow. Imagine hitting Lenny Bruce with a brick and making him read an old script from *90210*.

Here, listen in for a moment as Paris tells Nicky about the incident last week when our Humvee got stuck. I'll help out:

"Bitch, we were so totally clenched!"

My friend, we were afraid.

"Darnel was driving, and he was totally useless. Because of him our Hummer did a total FloJo in the Barrio, the bitch part."

The driver did not understand the car, it died suddenly in a neighborhood full of Hispanic gang members, who are known to be very dangerous.

"Then pussy-ass bitch Trey goes all award show."

The second of the two boys became visibly shaken and then cried.

"God, everyone will hear about it."

He will never have sex in this town again, ever.

"Of course N was totally pulling a total Judy G. The bitch was gone, useless."

I don't know why Nicole was so out of it.

"I'm so totally sick of that bitch. Really. She needs a wash. I'm dumping her ass."

But as a lifelong friend, I consider that to be part of her charm.

"It's time to blow this town and go to the Crater, there's a catwalk."

We are going to Manhattan for a few days, which was an unfortunate victim of a terrorist attack last year. I have a fashion show to attend. Pack accordingly.

"I gotta shoot rhubarb."

Pardon me, I must now depart to quickly defecate.

I have to listen to this all day long.

Nov. 29 | 02 Fairy Condescending

Oh, I just found out what a "Tinkerbell" is: she named me after a fairy. This chick named me after a fairy. You know, because I'm small. That's great, lady, thanks. Like I don't have to put up with enough shit from the other dogs in this town because I look more like a bug than a dog, now I get basically called a fag by people who think parking meters are some sort of metal plant that only grows in the city. Thanks so much. Your little Richie friend over there makes me redundant anyway; let me go for God's sake.

It's at least better than the other suggestions tossed around by her posse. I was almost "Mukluk," then I thankfully just barely missed "Ass Nugget." That Nicole Richie has some dry wit, eh? Sister Nicky cooled it up a tiny bit to "Tink," or "Tink Hilton," which has sort of a late '60s game-show host ring to it.

"The Twenty-Eight Million Dollar Cushion from All Reality," hosted by the lovely Tink Hilton!

Still, beats the pound.

DEC. 13 | 02 FASHION

I'm glad that you can't see me right now. We're headed to the Waldorf=Astoria hotel in Manhattan for a couple of days so Paris can do an interview for the big-deal fashion magazine *Avatar*, before we head off to Japan.

I've been dressed up for the trip to the airport in some sort of clown suit so pink and turquoise that even I can barely stand it, and I'm color-blind.

I have bells.

Bells.

Like I don't just naturally stick out enough, now I can annoy the deaf, too. Why not just go ahead and spray me with the juice of a skunk's ass and get the trifecta of offensive.

Rounding out the outfit are four custom-made booties that probably cost more than your car. It's hard enough to locomote on the Spanish tile with seven-inch legs, now my feet have all the grip of Spalding Gray watching *Schindler's List*.

Paris has a handful of other dogs here in LA with her and they're all larger than I am, so every five minutes one decides to play Pin the Jaws on the Tink and instead of escaping I spastically run in place like Scooby-Doo after seeing a ghost.

I'm so pissed off I don't know which shoes to take a shit in first.

DEC. 15 | 02 THE FLOOR

We've been here in the frankly awesome Waldorf=Astoria hotel in Manhattan for a couple of days now.

When it opened in 1930, this was the largest hotel in the world, and it's still easily one of the most impressive, with grand marble hallways, regal antechambers and foyers, and art deco design held from the time of its creation throughout.

Although all of the Hilton pads I've been to have been grand in one sense or the other, this is the first one that actually feels luxurious rather than merely expensive.

The Waldorf was the first to suggest that guests could live permanently in private suites. The Hilton sisters took their great grandpa up on this plan as kids, the whole of the thirtieth floor serving as the East Coast base of operations for all things Hilton while they grew up. Paris has her own place downtown now—our time here is more of a nostalgic layover for the day between here and Japan.

The decor in here is mostly untouched from the rest of the hotel's scheme. In fact, the first thing you really notice in the Hilton suite is the lack of personalization you'd expect from a pair of young permanent residents who in fact own the joint.

This lack of personal involvement with their surroundings becomes less confusing once you find yourself stuck listening in on phone conversations, as I am right now. Paris is trying in vain to understand something being described to her via cell phone by fellow millionaire heiress Casey Johnson.

Here, see for yourself:

"I forget. One of those heavy hot things that smooths out wrinkles."

That's an iron.

"No, on clothes. It's one of those heavy things that makes clothes smooth."

You mean an iron.

"It shoots, like, smoke."

Steam. You mean an iron.

"No, it's, like, flat. And totally heavy."

Look down at me, will you? Read my lips: I-R-O-N.

"No, for clothes. I don't know, you plug it in."

Is there a gas leak in here?

"No, that's for hair. This is for clothes. It's shaped like a piece of cake, but it's metal."

Jesus pole-vaulting Christ, woman, a 5-year-old child kno— IRON, IT'S AN IRON.

"No, but like heavy. God, what do you call that— stop barking, Tink. No, for clothes."

I don't know how much more of this I can take.

HOOVES

Shoes are everywhere. The 30th floor feels like you're in the lair of some sort of centuries-old dragon that the local villagers appease to keep it from burning up their town by sacrificing color-blind runway models to it. Dizzying.

WHAT'S IN ROOM 237, TONY?

Time with the Heiress has been mostly intermittent since we touched down in NYC and arrived at the hotel yesterday—she's been preoccupied with something. She did try to teach me to talk as you would a parrot by imitating simple phrases in my direction for an hour this morning, or I thought that's what was going on at the time; it turns out the Olsen twins were staying over last night and they got a little weird on Red Bull. They seem a little young for that sort of behavior to me, but then they seem a little young to be worth more than Belize and Switzerland combined.

While we're at it, let me tell you something very important about the Olsen twins: don't, under any circumstances, let them sleep over. I know, a lot of you sick people have been dreaming of that very thing, but that's only because you don't know any better. They seem to do everything together. *Everything*, including going for a pee. This they do in the middle of the night, walking to the bathroom, hand in hand.

Now, I don't know if you've ever seen Mary-Kate or Ashley up close and without the makeup, but at 3 a.m., a tiny pair of very pale girls walking hand in hand down a hotel hallway mumbling to themselves in that quiet nonsense-speak twins babble in is a lot to take, even if you've only seen the TV version of *The Shining*.

I was startled into emptying my bladder on a very expensive Persian rug from Shiraz. Fortunately, a bunch of porn stars also spent the night, so the blame for that was handily deflected.

Dec. 16 | 02 Spitelife

Manhattan.

We hit a new nightclub every night, it's exhausting.

Tonight's nightclub: Minge.

Minge seems to be following some sort of gynecology theme. All the chairs have stirrups and the dishes all have real cute names, Ovaries Over Easy, and like that. All the drinks have cranberry juice in them. Small order of Tater Tots, or as they would have it, "cysts": $24. If you order the house special, a large baked potato, it arrives at your table cranked open with a small speculum, which you get to keep as a souvenir. Clever.

Two weeks ago, apparently Minge was Gekko, a Wall Street–themed place that didn't have any chairs, just a lot of flat-panel TV screens hanging overhead like the stock exchange. Go to Gekko's bathroom, and you got somewhat roughly set up with a wire by fake FBI agents so you could go "entrap" your friends and giggle over the tape later. I think they were a little too committed to the gimmick with that one—the "feds" really worked a few kids over. There's a class-action suit pending. Still, it outlasted predecessor Fokus, a garden variety dance club that offered at-your-table LASIK surgery from a giant ceiling-mounted laser for $30. There's another class-action suit pending, as well as several patents.

The building started off its nightclub life as Barmageddon, which did okay for most of early 2001 with a post-apocalypse theme, falling out of favor after 9/11. "It's a year later and they're still on fire over there. We just can't compete with that." (Barmageddon manager Todd Hasenpfeffer's famous last quote before blowing town to set up a goth club in Miami, where he is reportedly still trying to find his way out of the airport.)

DEC. 17 | 02 RUMORS

We're in a weird nightclub called Luxuria—kind of an S&M theme, but with family restaurant–style food like potato skins and hot wings.

Nicky and Nicole joined us but have run off to leave Paris to her interview, the whole reason we're here tonight.

We find our interviewer alone at her own table off to a quieter corner of the Luxuria. Her name is Mina. Mina's current eyeliner level would allow her to Jane-Goodall a family of wild raccoons with no significant difficulty.

For a change, Paris is sipping a Red Bull and seems bored with both Mina and the interview before it even begins.

"So . . ." says Mina with a light smile, "I read in a tabloid that you spend a couple thousand dollars a month on tanning. Is this true?"

Paris, despite being otherwise alone at a table with a journalist, seems startled to be suddenly asked questions. To be fair, we *are* surrounded by people in latex gimp outfits taking orders for cheese stix.

Paris: "That isn't so much for once a month."

Mina: "Not for rent in Brooklyn, no."

Paris: "Well, in a way I'm renting the tan, right?"

Mina: "Well, okay. What are you up to next?"

Paris: "I'm off to Tokyo to promote my sister's line of handbags."

Mina: "Very good. Right . . . about fashion, then . . . I hear you design a lot of your own stuff."

Paris: "Fabulous, isn't it?"

Mina: "Did you design the outfit you have on now?"

Paris: "I did. Totally."

Mina: "Don't you think a miniskirt should have an ass?"

Paris: "I sit on it, what's the difference?"

Mina: "Fair enough. Now, you've come out in the past against fur and animal products."

Paris: "Animals are totally important."

Mina: "Right. But those are leather boots that you're wearing now."

Paris: "No, these are fake."

Mina: "I can see a brand on the bottom that plainly says 'one hundred percent real leather.'"

Paris: "I was told they were fake."

Mina: "You didn't look?"

Paris: "I can't see the bottom of my own feet, can I?"

Nicole Richie has suddenly just shown up like a fart in a car will when you're driving through both of the Carolinas and everyone has had a pecan log or two along the way.

Surely she can help make Paris less bitchy and clueless, saving this interview:

"Hey, wow, do you look like a raccoon on purpose?"

That's my girl.

DEC. 18 | 02 DEEP

It's like nine in the morning, and we're at the Waldorf gearing up for the airport.

On the phone just now:

"I just saw that movie *Gandhi*. If we really had people like that, then, like, the world would be very different."

She's almost cute sometimes.

On to Japan.

PERKS

One of the benefits of travel with the Heiress is being able to push the airlines around. Since we're going first class, I can take the trip by Heiress lap rather than drugged up and stuffed into a PortaPet cage to ride in the cargo hold like I heard Gia Carangi had to.

PARIS HILTON'S DEEPEST FEARS

A LIST, IN REVERSE ORDER OF GOOSEBUMP MAGNITUDE:

10. What if I say something stupid?

9. Constantly tanning might be revealed one day as somehow unhealthy.

8. The blue stuff in the gel mask is alive and getting it on with my face while I sleep.

7. Spa pee.

6. That cookie I ate when I was six.

5. The earth-killing giant asteroid scenario—there's just no way I can beat that thing for press coverage.

4. Exclamation marks and all caps are no longer allowed in e-mails.

3. The deformed Lionel Richie clay-head sculpture from that old video with the blind chick watching me outside my window at night.

2. See-through clothing no longer quite as see-through.

1. It's not a cold sore.

JAN. 11 | 03
HOW PARIS HILTON WILL ULTIMATELY CURE CANCER IN OUR LIFETIME

I have to admit, I never saw it coming. See, for Paris the only tricky bit was figuring out how to stop just the tumoral flesh from getting its supply of blood while leaving the other flesh unaffected.

Now, most oncologists look at the cell structure of the tumors, but the genius bit of what Paris had done was wisely figure that the secret lay not only in the structure, but in the *density* of those struct—

Okay, I'm done.

What she did do was just try to recharge her cell phone batteries in the microwave, which was, frankly, almost as cool to watch.

JAN. 21 | 03 DALLIANCES

About an hour ago I awoke on Paris's lap during a flight to see none other than the current Dalai Lama, or someone who looked a hell of a lot like him, seated across from us meditating.

"Hey, you're that guy!" Paris informed him.

"Correct," the Lama confirmed pleasantly back to her, eyes still closed.

"You, uh—" Paris snapped her fingers in an effort to jog her memory, each snap causing the Lama's serene face to twitch until his eyes popped open.

"—you, uh, can levitate or something, right?"

"No," the Lama managed with a serene smile, eyes closing once again back to his meditation.

"Yeah!" Paris continued, "you're like that spoon kid in *The Matrix*! Uh, 'there is no spoon,' right? Can you, like, bend shit? Oh, uh, I mean can you like bend *stuff*?"

The Lama opened his eyes again, sitting back in his seat, accepting that his meditation would be interrupted.

"Yes to both." He smiled at her.

"Really?!"

"No." He also smiled at her.

"Ah-ha! Good one, Sensei."

"Lama," his slight smile unbroken.

"Oh, right. Hey, why do they call you guys that? Why not a cool animal, like a shark? I'd rather be a shark than a llama."

The Lama, smile unbroken: "The shark, who can never stop moving or hunting, would enjoy being a llama for a day, I think. They graze and sleep in the sun all day."

"What? No way, llamas are totally gay . . . not you, I don't mean you're gay . . . wait, *are* there gay Lamas? You guys are eunuchs or something, aren't you?"

Still smiling: "We love all."

"Oh. I tried that. I got sore."

Now, it was fast enough to have been my imagination, but I *swear* I saw him grimace involuntarily at that image.

"Child, your manner is familiar to me. You are an American celebrity of some sort, aren't you?"

At this, Paris's face lit up.

"Paris Hilton." She extended her hand, which the Lama quickly accepted without hesitation; however, he had deftly wrapped his robe around his palm for the duration of the handshake in a way that she likely didn't notice.

This is a half-naked man who hugs lepers all day long for a living.

"Paris Hilton. I enjoy your hotels very much. You must like always having a home waiting for you, wherever you should go."

"Sure, it's bitchin'."

"Yes. Do you ever sleep outside?"

"Outside?"

"Yes."

"What with the bugs and stuff? Jesus, no."

"Do."

"What? Like, camping?"

"No. No tent. No blanket. You and the outside."

"Well, I've awakened like that before."

"Ah! And were you wiser that morning for it?"

"Well, I don't date Fred Durst anymore, if that's what you mean."

"It'll do."

The Lama settled back in his seat to meditate again, pleased enough with the encounter.

Paris leaned back into our seat, seemingly satisfied, and then she suddenly swooped around again toward the Lama.

"Hey"— she pushed against his shoulder, his eyes popping open again— "what do your friends call you?"

This time the smile faded to the scant remains of a grin, like when you've heard a good joke, but you're still waiting to get the results from a biopsy.

"Everyone is my friend, and all will call me as they understand me to be."

"Oh. But you have a name, right? It's like Salvador, or something, isn't it?"

The Lama's smile, still in place, was barely perceptible now.

"Tenzin, if you like, Paris Hilton."

"Oh, cool. Can I tell people I know that, or are you like undercover or something?"

"Yes."

"Hey, what's that one-hand-clapping thing about? In the woods or something?"

"They are not questions. They are puzzles, for you to work out. They are not about anything."

"Oh. Why?"

"Exactly."

"What?"

"Pardon me, Paris Hilton, I have to pee."

He never did come back to his seat.

THINGS THAT WILL TURN PARIS HILTON ON

A LIST, IN REVERSE ORDER OF MOJO:

5. Wind.

4. A sense of humor. By which I mean being tall enough to make other guys look funny.

3. The Washington Monument.

2. All those circus clowns crammed into that tiny, tiny car all at once like that.

1. Whoever it is that you're dating.

FEB. 05 | 03 THE PARIS HILTON EFFECT

We're on a plane headed back toward LA.

At the airport we seem to have picked up some celebrity lint—three of the guys from that band where they all try hard to look like the early '80s Billy Joel that Billy Joel himself tries real hard not to look like. We share a couple of rows of first-class seats.

Paris is awake; everyone else in the group is passed out. Paris keeps getting the stewardess to bring us things she doesn't want because the stewardess is very fat, and watching a fat stewardess having to angle and jiggle down the tiny aisle pointlessly every five minutes is better than the Russell Crowe movie now playing. Russell has gone too doughy to hold Paris's interest. It would seem Paris has got a lot of complexity when it comes to the algebra of figuring exactly what other people's fat means to her.

Now Paris is tossing peanuts at Nicky, who is not awake, but just awake enough to get pissed off and bat at the guitarist's face, who by this time is bleeding fairly freely from the nose, which is making the baby one seat up from him cry. The noise of the crying baby is waking the singer, who moans that as the public face of the band, they all need him to get his beauty sleep, and to stop pissing him off. To make his point, he unconsciously pitches an empty minibottle toward the source of his irritation—the baby. The bottle misses but gets the baby's mother upset enough to ring for the fat stewardess, who is by this time too tired from fetching pointless items for Paris all flight long to respond; this causes the mother to feel insufficiently serviced and to decree that she will not rest until the stewardess is fired and the singer is in jail.

Paris is flipping through an issue of *Vogue* with headphones on and is not even aware of the drama she's created four seats away. This seems to happen a lot— Paris leaves a wake of destruction just outside the tiny sphere of her awareness. She often seems like the starting point of one of those weird illustrative examples of Chaos Theory: Paris Hilton farts in an elevator in China, and an hour later all the elephants in the Bronx Zoo are mysteriously pregnant with baby penguins.

FEB. 16 | 03 TILL I DROP

I haven't made a journal entry in about two weeks. I've been too jet-lagged because I was busy serving as the hood ornament on some sort of last-days-of-Rome shopping orgy Paris has been on since we got back from Japan.

Previous shopping jags have been left out of my records because they're very dull for me. Generally, they go like this: Paris appears in some high-end store like the Visa messiah herself, the sales staff instantly recognize what's good for them and make with the ass-kissing so loaded with obsequiousness that it would embarrass Diane Sawyer, and then she spends the next hour or so throwing Pentagon-level cash at clothes, jewelry, and electronic trinkets.

The whole process can take as little as fifteen minutes or as long as six hours, but it's a leisurely experience done for its own sake, and all the rapidly uncooling trendy crap we take home for a brief stay in her closet before being thrown out is just sort of a by-product, like that rock concert T-shirt in your closet you only wear for irony after the band puts out that record their spouses helped them write.

It's not been that way recently. For the past two weeks the shopping has been a heavy-duty, almost ravenous experience. Paris will hit the usual high-end boutiques every morning, bask in the glow of the sales staff, and wallow in the admiration for a good two hours minimum, and then hit the lesser stores, presumably just to give the clerks who work there a good scare.

I never mention Paris's fiancé, Jason, despite the fact that we all technically live in the same house, because whenever Paris is with him I'm left on my own, but I think they've had a fight or something and this might be a distraction.

Or, I thought so until this morning when I overheard Paris tell Nicky that she got a tip that she's got more tabloid heat than usual, with a small staff recently assigned to her and only to her. That's right: somewhere in Hollywood, some paparazzi guy goes to a bar every night to drink off the effects of his long hard day working on the Paris Hilton Squad. Instead of seeing this total intrusion as unpleasant, Paris seems to see this as a significant step up and is putting on a deliberate show for them with a lot of glamorous consumption.

Or, perhaps she just awoke one morning and realized she had more cash than Al Pacino in *Scarface*, decided to stop living in all this poverty she has been putting up with, and go get those four hundred pairs of shoes one really needs to get through a month.

Frankly, I wish she'd just leave me at home for this, because not only is the raw gluttony hard to watch, but while doing it she's taken to talking to me as if I can understand her.

I mean, obviously I can understand her, but I don't register it, because who the hell wants a master who knows you understand what "don't" means.

Anyway, lately Paris has been theorizing out loud to me while we shop. Turns out shopping is a very nuanced situation, and you, not being her, are probably doing it wrong. This really deserves to be its own entry, hang on:

LARGESSE 101

As far as I have been able to follow without passing out while being told, the math of shopping like a socialite seems to boil down to three basic actions:

First, all stores—all of them—have better stuff in them somewhere than they're showing you. Well, not *you*, everyone else. You're special, and you're not twisting the valve on the cash fire hose until you see the good stuff.

This has proven amusing for me, because although it may or may not be true in the high-end boutiques where everything, and I mean everything—right down to who gets what ply of tissue in which employee bathroom—has a sort of pecking order to it, it has absolutely nothing to do with the reality in the average strip mall store, which simply only has room for what it has to offer.

Less experienced sales clerks will try to reason with Paris when she demands to see the good stuff; the more savvy simply take her to the storeroom in back where nothing has a price tag on it yet, then charge her five times retail.

The particularly experienced clerks will avoid the usual stock completely and fish something defective out of the returns pile, making claims along the lines of, "See, it's supposed to have one large and one small armhole—it's fresh from LA . . . the gang members do that to their stuff so they can shoot easier, and Givenchy appropriated it for next season. Shall I ring it up so you can get the jump on it?"

Of course, someone then sees Paris wearing it outside a film premiere and it becomes a self-fulfilling fashion prophecy—so it sort of works out on both ends.

The second thing Paris has figured out in her shopping is that the way to be certain of top-quality service is to let them know who is boss right away. This is less of a money-throw-around issue like above, and more of a "let's automatically reject the first five things the clerk says" maneuver.

A recent example:

Paris: "I want these Manolo Blahniks in a ten."

Clerk: "Of course. You know, we do keep your size on file, Miss Hilt—"

Paris: "I didn't say I wanted whatever is on your file, I said I want these shoes in a ten."

Clerk: ". . . er, right. We have them."

Paris: "In brown?"

Clerk: "The ones you're holding are brown."

Paris: "That's not what I'm asking, do you have these in brown?"

Clerk: "Let me get them for you."

Paris: "Stop right there!"

It's more about power than logic. Again, it works better with people being paid to tolerate it—the same control tactic pulled in a chain store tends to get the surreptitious slide-index-finger-in-between-buttocks-and-paint-credit-card-with-butt-sweat-when-I-give-this-witch-her-change maneuver from the clerks.

The third, and much more simple, rule of shopping would appear to be the axiom that goes something like, "Since I can afford to grab absolutely all of this shit and keep other people from having it the same time as I do, I'm going to do it."

Feb. 19 | 03 All Aboard

Currently I'm at some party of about twenty-five or so semifamous people happening in a grand Spanish villa–style mansion in Beverly Hills.

Paris is currently bopping around the pool topless, a good description of both outfit and psyche. She's had about nine of those little Red Bull cans in the past hour . . . when she does finally pee, she's going to carve the porcelain of the toilet just like one of those chainsaw guys making an ice sculpture.

Paris's interaction with the boys here is an interesting spectacle to watch: she doesn't do anything but dance alone in some corner, then all the guys sort of find their way to her, one at a time, like bees. She'll humor them individually for a bit, then with instant and complete dismissal the guy is given the boot. The guy then wanders off, looking as if he'd gone to a guillotine by way of a kissing booth.

Despite all this going on in plain sight of everyone, the steady flow of boymeat never slows down even a little, which makes it hard to pity any of them even slightly.

Hmmm . . . some reality-show semifamous dweeb has been floating facedown in the pool for quite some time now. I thought she was pulling a stunt, but a crowd gathered around her about fifteen minutes ago and now it looks like a pair of paramedics are here; so either she overdid the refreshments, or she's really committed to the joke.

Oh, the glamour.

Huh. About thirty feet from the pool there's another body in the grass.

I don't really follow rock music so I don't know who that is facedown in the garden, dead to the world.

Or possibly just dead. I can't tell, but she is covered in ants.

Nope, slight movement.

It's a drag when there's only enough medical concern in the room for one and you've got two dying clichés in attendance.

Not bound by such concerns, I stopped typing long enough to go pee on her head. She revived just enough to roll her face out of her own vomit puddle and avoid pulling a Jimi here on the lawn.

FEB. 21 | 03 THEY BOUGHT IT

We're back in LA.

Ah, well, mission accomplished. Paris's shopping gambit seems to have paid off; I see the good little tabloids have her various recent bi-coastal shopping sprees well documented. Now Paris is the Outrageous Spendy Heiress for the foreseeable future—bankable space filler until Michael Jackson does something else weird.

"Oh, don't you envy it!" they scream. "Oh, the life of the Heiress!"

I've noticed that tabloids and e-mail spammers use exactly the same wording and punctuation.

We're reading all about ourselves in the back of a limo, making our way back to the LA house from a photo shoot Paris did for *Amenorrhea* magazine, a hip new venture aimed at the young model community, which is perhaps a little sick of people passing judgment on its lifestyle . . . or, as the community describes itself: "amenorrhea: dry humor for today's fashion model."

Paris knows the editor, who is fresh out of intensive care and eager to kick ass in the world of magazine publishing.

FEB. 24 | 03 KICKS

Paris has been quiet in the week that has passed since the birthday parties in Las Vegas.

Whatever has happened, Jason is rarely at the LA house anymore.

Paris just put down the tabloid article she was reading about herself and asked the limo driver whether there is a minivan with shaded windows following us. After glancing in the rearview mirror he confirmed that there was, and with a grin she cooly told him to make way to Cole Haan shoes on Rodeo.

Gah. More stunt shopping for the rags.

We arrive in the shoe store to find Star Jones of *The View* tasking a small group of sales people to slap some shoes on her that feature straps but won't make her feet look like a pair of breast implants being pushed through a tennis racket. The saleswoman currently servicing her feet is perspiring heavily, with a small mound of rejected choices accumulating behind her. Another stands off to the corner visibly shaken, likely the recipient of an earlier tongue lashing.

They're earning their cash today. When two of them simultaneously spot us entering, they nearly break an ankle trying to beat each other to us.

Breathlessly, in both the literal and figurative sense, they ask in unison: "What can we do for you today, Miss Hilton?"

Paris smiles here, knowing her reply in advance. She makes a vague hand gesture toward the entire display.

"This, in tens."

"Er—which."

"You have other showrooms?"

" Er . . . no."

"In tens, please."

Over by the small row of seats, we hear Star Jones suck in her breath. Well, in fact we feel our respective body hairs pulled toward her more than we hear anything. My ears pop.

"Guuuuuuuuuuuuuuurl!" she purrs admiringly.

Paris only smiles wanly at the room.

"Can't really ever have enough shoes, can you?"

With that, she handed the sales manager who had come out to greet her personally her credit card, jokingly told him to "be gentle," and said they could deliver the shoes at their convenience to her LA address.

I don't know if Paris even likes these shoes. Hardly matters: her work here is done.

I like how someone who can't work a toaster without causing a third-degree burn can engineer both continued solid tabloid coverage for the next month, and a for-certain mention and likely guest appearance on a popular national television show all in one fell swoop in under five minutes.

PARIS HILTON'S FAVORITE INDULGENCES

A LIST, IN REVERSE ORDER OF GRATIFICATION:

5. Threatening the help with immigration until they're able to put on the level of quality impromptu talent show that stays with you long after you see it.

4. Pulling up next to a herd of middle-aged soccer moms and just watching them twitch.

3. A lake and a bucket of skippin' diamonds.

2. Quietly bankrolling Ryan Seacrest's career. That's right, she hates you all just that much.

1. The quiet sense of pride I get from being able to fit inside a Slinky.

MAR. 26 | 03 ANGER MANAGEMENT

We're in a trendy seafood restaurant in Hollywood being interviewed by a gossip magazine guy with no hint of eyebrows and a huge soul patch on his chin, which in terms of crafty hair maneuvering makes Sam Donaldson look like Niccolo Machiavelli. I can't tell if he's fresh from chemotherapy, going for a look, or just really enjoys watching bacon cook.

Paris seems about as interested in him as an Amish carpenter would be with one of those Tamagotchi digital key ring pets.

Guy: "So. Why don't you tell me what happened with Shannen Doherty?"

Odd, nasally voice he has.

Paris: "Well, I wasn't there, so I don't know for certain, but I figure the obstetrician sneezed while gripping her head with the forceps or something."

Guy: "What?"

Paris: "Her eyes?"

By way of illustration, Paris made two fists here, then put one on her cheek and the other on her temple.

Guy: "No, I mean the fight outside the club Deluxe."

Paris: "What fight?"

Guy: "Well, I read she punched you and then pelted your car with eggs and screamed at you in the parking lot."

Paris: "Oh, that. Actually, she punched the empty air about two feet in front of Ed Begley Jr."

Guy: "Really?"

Paris: "Then she totally pelted the car two cars to the left of us, screamed at a stop sign to keep its damn hands off Rick, throttled a shrub for a little, wobbled around, and walked face-first into a parked Escalade."

Guy: "Right."

Paris: "I figure for her it's like when you try to look at your own nose, or whatever. You'd think her agent would get her a dog or something. I don't know how she gets anywhere on her own."

Guy: "Right . . . well, she isn't actually cross-eyed, she's just got a slight unevenness, which wouldn't really effect her vis—"

Paris: "Maybe a monkey. One of those helper monkeys."

Guy: "Right. So, well, I have to ask . . . *did* you sleep with her husband Rick Salomon while they were hooked up?"

Paris: "Oh, absolutely not."

Guy: "Then how does all this tabloid stuff get started?"

Paris: "I dunno. The tabloids are always saying weird shit about me. Besides, he's like covered in back hair, which is too gross."

Guy: "Back hair?"

Paris: "Like a marmot. I don't find that sexy."

Guy: "Huh? Well, how's Ed looking these days?"

Paris: "Pleased with himself."

Guy: "Right. Well, then there is the other recent Deluxe story, where you allegedly verbally attacked Sarah Howard."

Paris: "Who?"

Guy: "The actress Sarah Howard . . . you once costarred with her briefly in a bit part . . . evidently you didn't like her talking to your former fiancé Jason Shaw, and you called her names from across the bar."

Paris: "That never happened."

Guy: "Says here you 'grabbed Sarah by the hair and bounced her head off the table repeatedly like Tito Puente on a pair of bongos.'"

Paris's eyes rolled here.

Paris: "Does that even *sound* true?"

Well, she has a point. I wasn't there that night, I can't confirm or deny anything, but it does explain this bloody clump of hair she keeps in her change purse.

Guy: "Well, witnesses imply you may have had a few drinks."

Paris: "I don't drink."

Guy: "Well, okay. Now, another rumor floating around is that you actually pay the owners of these establishments to clue you in when personal rivals show up."

Paris: "What?"

Guy: "The theory is that they enjoy the free press of the catfights, and your cash, and that you enjoy the free press and getting the jump on your enemies. Any comment on that?"

Paris rolled her eyes even more dramatically, then sort of slumped her head down on the table, such was the weight of her exasperation with this goofy line of questioning.

Then:

Paris: "What are you—like—high? Listen. I don't want trouble, I don't want to be known as trouble, I just want to hang out with my friends, and these crazy people somehow find me."

Guy: "Okay then. Next question—"

Paris picked me up and concluded the interview in sign language before turning on her heel and heading for the door.

Why does she keep agreeing to do these interviews?

HOW PARIS HILTON ALLEGEDLY WINS IN AN ALLEGED BAR FIGHT, ALLEGEDLY

A LIST, IN REVERSE ORDER OF BAD MOTOR SCOOTERNESS:

5. "What bar fight? She totally made that shit up. I was in Africa, drinking a non-alcoholic beer and reading the Bible to legless orphans with AIDS."

4. Weaken and confuse your opponent beforehand from across the room. Everything is a potential missile: keys, ashtrays, shot glasses, shoes, and if you're quick enough, Deryck Whibley.

3. Nobody argues for very long with a lighter and a can of hairspray. Even if the other girl does win the fight, she ain't going home to her cats pretty.

2. Be sure you're really that angry to begin with. Count to five. A chin implant knocked to the other side of your face is hard to live down.

1. Any sensei will tell you: the smartest fight is the one you don't have. If you see Jason Shaw or think he might be stopping by, simply avert your eyes and leave the room. It's just that easy.

Mar. 30 | 03 What I Would Love

Just one day out of the week when I don't have to smell heiress armpit all day long.

April 08 | 03 Beep Beep

NYC—My first runway fashion show.

I have never seen this many models at once before. I did once see a Día de los Muertos parade in LA, that was pretty close, only much more chipper.

Everyone backstage is tense with pre-catwalk anticipation, except for the actual models, who all seem to be in the same mental place Paris is in when acquaintances are trying to get her attention. I look at them and imagine that white empty void where Morphus first explains about the Matrix to Keanu, but instead of the two of them in red leather chairs, it's a bunch of tall, thin, bored models standing around not talking to each other and smoking.

In fact, Paris is easy to lose back here. She normally sort of looks like a giraffe in the monkey house, but here she's just another thin blade of oddly dressed grass with a blank expression in a lawn of the same.

The smell of industrial-strength hairspray and hastily vomited-up rice cakes is overwhelming.

Hey, I did meet the nicest person about an hour ago—one of those rare souls

who sort of makes even boring empty stuff like this seem worthwhile . . . some woman in public relations I think, I can't remember her name.

See, I got separated from Paris and then lost in the crowd while she was backstage, which was a little freaky because everyone was looking absolutely everywhere but at their feet, and I could have been trampled under countless stiletto heels very easily. This woman must have known Paris and recognized me as belonging to her. She scooped me right up, gave me a cracker with some foie gras on it, and took me right backstage to Paris, who was deeply relieved. Even when the stage manager didn't recognize her at first, even though she clearly expected that he would, and he made her wait while he had to look her name up before letting her go backstage, she remained bouncy and effervescent the whole time. It was frankly inspiring. I wish I had taken better note of her name; I think it was Lizzie something or other. So patient and kind. You rarely meet people that even tempered and in control of themselves in the big city.

April 11 | 03
MTV Network Building, Times Square

Paris is here to help promote her television show on VH1, a television show that technically doesn't exist yet and won't begin shooting for another month.

The cavernous main studios are surpassingly large inside, like a warehouse. Stretching from one end of the room to the other are rows of small cubicles just large enough for one or two people, a dense honeycomb-like hive of reality television people, pop culture journalists, film critics, stand-up comedians . . . anyone with a face recognizable enough to serve as a talking head—all stuffed into small, closet-sized cubicles painted the shade of green that can be digitally removed, with televisions placed directly in front of their respective cubicles to directly feed the personalities inside images for their approval or critique.

A giant white board with one word printed upon it in three-foot-high black letters hovers behind the televisions, but in front of the producers and other people, giving the hired heads of the day one constant, guiding direction: IRONY.

A sea of bemused smirks delivers the goods, twenty-four hours a day, seven days a week, all recorded and ready for broadcast within minutes.

Some of the faces seem out of place, not yet popular enough for this task, unrecognizable. We are told their tapes will be aired after their respective shows are created, become hits, and they are suitably loved by the public.

We fall into this group, which is convenient, because our taping session will be relatively short, and this place is seriously weirding me out. It feels like a convenience store does at 3 a.m., very bright and disorienting . . . only vast and with Sting playing in the background.

We share a green cubicle, Nicole, Paris, and myself. Rock videos, clips of television shows, and the late '70s William Shatner low-budget horror movie *Kingdom of the Spiders* all stream in for critique with seemingly no connection between them.

We are told to just relax and comment on whatever, say whatever we like, but the IRONY sign is always visible past the glow of the set.

Paris asks Nicole what that sign means; she thought irony was when something is opposite, or something.

Nicole shrugs. "They want us to pretend to hate stuff, I think."

"Oh."

We silently watch the movie for a while. Fifteen minutes later, Paris nudges Nicole again.

"Then why don't they put HATE on the sign?"

Nicole rolls her eyes.

"That'd be weird, bitchnuts. Hate is bad."

"Oh."

A warmly smiling producer pokes her head into our cubicle.

"Don't worry about being ironic, girls, we have Mo Rocca in today. Why, just his bow tie and glasses are irony enough for one hundred VH1s."

Nicole and Paris returned the sweet smile to the producer and watched the movie some more, falling asleep about halfway through.

CHEESE

It's a few hours after my last entry. We're all sort of ready to leave now, but Paris and Nicole have to shoot a promo for their show, the concept and name of which is still being discussed. The girls are standing around in front of a large blank screen that will be replaced with whatever is appropriate for the show, just as soon as there is one.

An unseen and disembodied voice offers direction:

"We'll keep it general girls, just fake it."

"Okay."

"Before the interview we want to film some short bits of you two standing around to insert in stuff later. Strike a few poses, will ya?"

Nicole rolls her eyes and makes a bored, put-upon face that I would do a lot if I had a face that could make expressions.

"Perfect!" yells the disembodied voice.

The fact of her getting something right and henceforth being cooperative with her tormentors causes Nicole to crack a wide, contrarian smile instead.

"Better!"

Nicole sighs a defeated sigh. Paris throws on a trucker cap and strikes one of her many stock fashion model poses.

"Hot!" calls the same voice, still unseen. "Love the hat! Irony!"

"Really?!" Paris seems pleased to have done something so effortlessly right.

"Sex it up a little!"

Both Nicole and Paris whip off their tops instantly. Nicole has half unbuttoned her jeans before the nervously laughing voice woahs! them to stop.

"I just meant make pouty faces. We're a family network here."

"So, imply oral, but not vaginal sex?"

"Bingo."

The two re-dressed and did as instructed. Paris paused to lift me up to face level to get me involved in the images.

Again I curse my lack of facial dexterity, but I really tried my best to snarl.

"Okay, just respond to our statements or questions naturally! Don't perform, don't over-think."

Thought you said they should be natural.

"What was the best part of your adventure?"

"When?"

"What adventure?"

A barely audible sigh escaped from behind the lights.

"Your show, girls, what was the best part?"

After a pause for the idea to settle in, Nicole leveled her gaze right at the camera; with utter and complete sincerity and in a level voice she said:

"I really valued this time to grow, to learn about myself, to face challenges and to grow and to learn from them."

Nicole leaned back on her heels, very pleased with both her answer and its delivery.

I swear, if you squinted, for a minute she was Sting himself, it was pretty impressive.

APRIL 23 | 03 NEIGHBORS

The LA house remains sort of large for one permanent occupant. Unfortunately, Paris has opted to fill it with animals, which I enjoy just about as much as you do when the yard outside your house decides it wants to fill the empty spaces in its life with army ants.

Paris already has three Pomeranian dogs, possibly the world's most stupid animal not featured on *That '70s Show*, for me to contend with, which I do mostly by letting them chase me toward a wall on the hard tile, and then simply leaping onto a bit of carpet for traction. I stop, and they make a satisfying crunching noise and can't find the food dish for a week.

They're actually starting to walk funny. I would just reason with them dog to dog, but it's like talking to a brick.

Sometimes Paris gets kooky, and it's not dogs that mysteriously show up, it's serious shit, like a baby tiger. I don't know who keeps trying to tame these jungle-based animals, I don't know what you think they're going to do for you that a simple dog won't, but it's hell on earth for a domesticated animal to have to deal with something that understands everything in terms only of survival.

Me: "Uh . . . do you want a biscuit, too? I'm going to the kitchen."

It : *"Don't look me in the eyes, I'll kill you, do you understand?"*

Thanks, whoever puts jungle cats on the same pet market as us small defenseless dogs, it's a joy.

APRIL 25 | 03 BACON

Back at the toy dog breeder where I grew up, another Chihuahua and I once watched a flood wipe out a town on TV. Since the other Chihuahua believed in God and I don't, I asked him why he thought God would allow that sort of thing to happen. I expected one of those floaty leap-of-faith sort of answers you tend to get when you ask people about their religious views, but instead I got a shrug and a nonchalant "If you were a god, and you got bored, you'd do the same thing on occasion."

Makes sense to me. Think about it, if you get stuck outside your house with nothing to do, and there are a lot of ants around, what would happen to the ants?

Probably something a lot like what happens to the guys that show up at Paris's house parties.

I don't know why Paris looks like she's thinking about hooking that car battery up to that guy's metal nipple rings, why he's cool with that, or what they think could possibly happen besides the obvious, but I'm just going to get a jump on things and dial 911 now.

April 26 | 03 Serve Cold

I awoke from a short nap to find Nicole Richie giggling and pointing at me in a way that I instantly didn't like. Others gathered around, also giggling. I caught sight of myself in a mirror over the wet bar.

In white baby powder someone had written TURD on my side. Because I'm small and brown, see.

Hilarious.

A small plastic baggie of that same baby powder quietly stashed in whatever Richie carry-on item I can get to before we leave for the airport is going to make the upcoming flight to Manhattan pretty hilarious, I can tell you that.

April 27 | 03 ☉H

Well, the powder gag worked, although not as well as I would have liked.

I can't tell for sure, but I think Nicole was actually upset with the airport's cavity search woman for using lube.

Unbelievable.

APRIL 30 | 03 BIG DEAL

Well, I attended my very first video awards show.

It's a lot like going to the vet: everyone, basically, is there just trying to see nipples, they keep shining bright lights at you, and the music sucks at both.

APRIL 31 | 03 COCONUT GROVE, Miami

I awoke this morning to find one of the many hard-to-identify C-list celebs who routinely fill out the dance card passed out on the floor, near a puddle of vomit. I think this one is from that reality show where you do all kinds of crazy crap for the joy of looking amazingly gullible and submissive on national television. She has scorpion stings all over her face.

Here's the thing: the vomit had no food in it, only about a bottle of vodka and a half-dozen Weebles. That's right, Weebles—those little egg-shaped dolls from the '70s or whenever that wobble but don't tip over.

Must have been quite an evening. Whatever she was auditioning for, I'm sure she got it.

MAY 02 | 03 NEW

Say, want to know how my morning went? Well, I'll tell you: I just spent twenty minutes (that's an hour and a half in dog minutes) watching Lady Einstein here try to stuff a one hundred–dollar bill into a vending machine.

"You don't know that I don't want that much soda!" she actually yelled at it, before calling it "a complete retread." I think she meant "retard," but who knows.

She's in the other room sulking and drinking from the tap. I spent the rest of the morning trying to lick a power socket.

MAY 03 | 03 FABULOUS

Nicole, Paris, and I are staying here in some palace that Tony Montana would have envied while Paris poses for somebody with a funny name who is marketing a new line of something or other. Mainly she seems to be here so she can call white guys with dreadlocks "bitchnuts." This they will unconvincingly pretend to find cute, which is a good place to note Paris's interesting effect on men. Straight guys will hit on her relentlessly, which is a whole other book, but will ultimately sort of bottleneck each other in the rush-over and fail to make much of a connection. Her real success is with gay men, who react to her like they're the monkeys and she's the fabulous monolith come to teach them how to kill things with bones. By "gay" I don't mean gay as in merely homosexual in orientation, I mean the kind of gay that can ruin a Thanksgiving. To people so attuned, Paris is irresistible: on the one hand possessed of undeniable massive quantities of Fabulous, and on the other always about three minutes away from a Judy Garland–style train wreck the likes of which would make the real Judy Garland seem like the mustachioed drag queen version of Judy Garland.

MAY 05 | 03 TALKING TO HERSELF

Heh . . . stumbled across Paris's daily schedule last night. A short excerpt:

11 A.M.

Awake. Size up person next to you. If pretty, gently awaken and offer breakfast. If the product of dim club lights, dial #6 on the house line, and await his or her removal.

11:15 A.M.

Shower. Retain used water for buyparishiltonsusedbathwater.com.

Love those guys.

12:00 P.M.

Select trucker hat for the day. Attempt to balance mocking the poor with looking jaunty.

Remember: You don't want too much irony but you don't want too little either.

1:00 P.M.

Call Olsen twins. Observe progress.

Try, once again, to talk them out of attending college.

If anything happens to me, the lifestyle must live on. They are the best last hope.

MAY 08 | 03 *THE SIMPLE LIFE*

Good to finally be typing again . . . I haven't been able to keep notes for about a week.

Once we arrived on the set of *The Simple Life*, all of Paris's cell phones were inactive, and the one I happen to prefer was the only one she could get a signal on. It was the small-craft weather advisory service, but Paris seemed to need to call it about 500 times a day anyway, like a kind of cell phone nicotine gum.

Now that we can't get that either, I've got my toy back.

Nicole, Paris, the main two on-set producers for *The Simple Life*, and what's gotta be an actor who is portraying a character named Trae Lindley are all seeing us to our new room in the one and only hotel in the area. The last room had something in the walls that was making Paris cough, which eventually interrupted shooting.

Looking out the window, at first I thought our new room was next to an oil tanker or something, but it turns out that was just the sky.

The new room has smells in it that I can't relay very easily to you without biting you in your crotch. I'll say this, I sort of pine for the old one, which didn't have a window and smelled like fresh bleach.

This hotel, and us with it, is, by the way, in what I hope isn't Altus, Arkansas, but has gotta be, like, a small, vaguely crumbling ex-Soviet empire province of Estonia, right on the gulf of Finland.

Producer number two, like many of the people we've met here in Estonia, is ex-navy. Producer number one is actually former Russian army. This has made for an interesting shoot since these two were possibly trying to kill each other sometime before 1991 when the Soviet Union collapsed and Estonia took the chance to be its own unoccupied independent country again. The two producers have put the majority of their past behind them to work together as one in the effort to make Paris and Nicole flinch every five minutes by booming slightly defensive claims at them.

"Estonia is being now big country! Growing! We have thirty-three ships in Merchant Marine!"

However, at this claim a slight argument broke out when producer number two dared to correct producer number one—apparently one of the ships is actually a personal yacht docked under the Estonia flag to avoid some sort of legal trouble back home. Nobody local is allowed anywhere near it, and so it shouldn't count. There was a brief period of maniacal screaming, then the actor who portrays Trae Lindley, whose name I can never catch but is something that sounds like a Klingon choking on gum, yelled something that shut up the two producers immediately. After a moment of terse pin-drop silence, number one spoke to Paris and Nicole in his version of English:

"We bring you to your room, eh? You get dinner, then sleep. No bouncy bouncy, eh? We shoot all the bar scenes tomorrow! Is goot! Done quick!"

"Done quick!" repeated number two to no one in particular, as if his name had been roll-called.

"Done quick" is the mantra on set, and it is well adhered to.

It turns out after a quick meeting with the two stars, Fox decided to keep the budget for this show as thrifty as possible. The interior scenes are being shot in a soundstage about the size of a small warehouse . . . exactly the size of a small warehouse, since that's what it was until two weeks ago, here in Estonia with local actors.

The exterior shots will be done in a couple of days in Arkansas.

Total Estonian shoot time? Six days. We're on day five.

"So . . . uh . . . what's for dinner?" Nicole nervously ventured.

Of the cast and crew of *The Simple Life*, only producer number one speaks any English, and he seems to understand less than he speaks. It's not hard to set him off. Both of these guys look like Stalin, very intense. Both seem to enjoy the nerves they clearly inspire in the girls.

"Ah!" Producer number one's eyes developed a proud glint. "Western food is very popular here! You enjoy all varieties of Power Bar, eh? We even have newest flavor, Choco-berry! Forty-two krooni a piece. Fresh, eh?"

Nicole made an involuntary face and leaned over to Paris.

"What is that in, like, real money?"

"I dunno— What the fuck is a krooni?"

Producer number one, clearly preoccupied with something else, waved their concerns away with his hand while the two of them made for the door.

"You get sleep now! We finish tomorrow! Then you punch cow!"

"What?"

"Punch cow! Dead!"

It wouldn't be the first time inelegant English has lead to false expectations since we've been here, but I really want to see Paris have to punch out a cow.

With the two Stalins gone, that leaves us with Trae or whoever.

The Estonian actor, or whoever, like the rest of the family actors, speaks perfect English, but only what's on his script; he understands not one word.

He smiled at the two girls, snagged one of the pillows off of the bed, and lay flat on the floor. Vigorous snoring followed. Despite half-hearted flirting from both girls, the actor has actually been married for about a decade with about a dozen kids and is not much interested in Paris or Nicole . . . or anything but the green card Fox will score for him should the show do okay. Evidently he'll be a part of some other fake news event with Paris to promote this thing, but they haven't decided what yet.

Nicole and Paris are now shivering together in the one bed in the room and complaining about really not wanting to have to punch a cow.

MAY 10 | 03 ALTUS, ARKANSAS

Since my last notes in Estonia we've flown nonstop to Arkansas to run around a few real farms and shoot exteriors for the show.

I don't know how all of this will look anything even remotely like real, but Fox claims to know what they're doing. Hard to argue with their reality show ratings.

With the pair of scary Stalinesque producers left behind to bicker over details in Estonia, we've been introduced to a sort of bitchy queenlike individual, in charge of the domestic exterior shoot.

If he ever should make it to the other side of a camera, he would set back gay rights in this country to whatever they were like around about 1805 in Wyoming.

This has been the most mind-blowing day of the shoot so far: after a full day of nothing but walking out of buildings, which we never entered any farther than the front door, and being screamed at because we weren't doing it naturally enough, Paris is now standing out in a field, with two grips or interns or whatever you call them holding on to her arm.

"Okay, do it honey!" our new director bellows through a completely unnecessary megaphone, which serves only to make him sound like he is directing us from the fast-food drive-thru window across the street. He was in fact much easier to hear without the bullhorn, but he refuses to let go of it.

By "it," Paris is being directed to push her outstretched arm forward into the pair of grips who are there to provide resistance. What they are doing is setting up the shot that I'm guessing will someday be a fairly famous scene in which Paris's arm somehow inseminates a cow . . . or interrogates it, or something. I think they're going figure that one out later, after they add the cow digitally.

"Too fast!" screeches the gay drive-thru voice. "Slower! Slower! More resistance! This is a very young cow, honey!"

I seriously need to get out of this life. The streets were rough, but I understood what was going on most of the time.

NOV 23 | 03 BLUE TAPE BLUES

Okay, nightmare scenario: try to imagine that you've been working . . . right, check that—occasionally putting forth some effort—toward cultivating a public image of some sort.

You've been sort of doing this on and off for a couple of years now and finally, after months of asking very nicely every now and again, you get your own show on a major network. Mainstream celebrity; it's just within your grasp. The show is about to premiere, the buzz is good, things are looking up.

Then suddenly, out of the blue, every rumor that you've paid a small nation of publicists to dispel over the years becomes crystallized by some sleazy figure from your past who you wouldn't have anything to do with under normal circumstances, except for that one time when you did some of the hairier bits from the Kama Sutra with him in front of a camera.

What do you do? You then select the slickest, oiliest spinmeister you can, and when Scott McClellan says no, you get the next guy on the list, and you ask for his advice.

If you're Paris Hilton, you actually have someone do that for you, and then you show up at eight in the morning not yet very awake in a jogging suit with your parents and small dog in tow.

You sit quietly with your head tilted down toward your knees, and then the four of you have more or less the following conversation:

Publicist: "So. This thing real? That you in there?"

Paris: " Y—"

Dad: "Don't answer him honey."

Publicist: "Er . . . I'm not a defense attorney. I don't need a presumption of innocence to proceed, what I need is to know what I'm trying to spin here. We're all on the same side."

Mom: "Let's just assume that it needs your attention."

Publicist: "Okay. And this Salomo—"

Mom: "Don't use the name, please."

Publicist: ". . . Right. This fella—are you in any kind of communication with him right now?"

Dad: "Not directly."

Paris: " I had Tink fart in an envelope and I mailed it to him, if that counts."

Publicist: "Well—"

Paris: "It was Nicole's idea."

Publicist: "Yes. Let's not do that anymore. Instead let's get a grip on what this thing's distribution is going to be."

Paris: "It's all over the Internet—"

Dad: "Shh. Don't use that word."

Publicist: "What, the Intern—?"

Dad: "Shh."

Publicist: "Okay. So, uh, it's out there, and it's pretty clearly and undeniably you in the film."

Paris: "Yes."

Mom: "Shhh."

Paris: "What?"

Dad: "Don't."

The publicist slumped back in his chair at this.

Publicist: "All right, listen, we're pretty clearly the exploited here. This is not going to be hard to handle."

Mom: "So how do we react publicly?"

Publicist: "Well, you're shocked and dismayed, of course."

Paris raised her hand as one might in school.

Paris: "Uh, I don't do shocked and dismayed. I'm going to need training. A lot of it."

The publicist involuntarily shot up straight in his seat, tried to fake, like, his enthusiasm was not the new Manhattan apartment he just envisioned buying but instead was an itch on his back, and then settled back down in one fairly smooth motion.

Both parents wanted to glare at Paris for a moment here, I think, but didn't want to upset her more than she was, so they let it pass. For her part, Paris was cool as usual. She was, in fact, playing a Game Boy she had hidden in her jogging suit with the sound off, and had been since 6 a.m. She was doing very well and didn't want to pause.

Publicist: " All right, then, we'll simply shoot for 'dismayed' rather than 'shocked.' Keep it quiet, and we'll let the public know anyone near this tape is being sued into a bloody pulp."

Both parents nod approvingly at this course of action.

Publicist: "Paris, honey, have you ever considered dating a nice Amish gentleman?"

Paris: "Steven Spielberg?"

Publicist: "He's Jewish, dear. The Amish are a bunch of farmers in Pennsylvania. They're a very technology-resistant people, they don't have any cameras. If this has really happened so many times, well, these guys wouldn't keep taping you."

Paris looked up from her Game Boy, still hidden.

Paris: "Really?"

Publicist: "Sure. Plenty buff, too—"

Paris gave him her fullest attention—

Publicist: "—They work all day, very har . . ."

Paris's face returned to her lap.

"Oh."

Mom and Dad patted her back comfortingly. While things were dealt with as well as they could be, Paris quietly beat the eighth level of BloodNinja IV.

MAY 07 | 04 GRAND UNIFICATION BLEARY

It's always appealing to think that you're witnessing the apocalypse.

I think everybody does it at some point. You awaken, look around you, and your mind gets its circuits blown by a glimpse into something so mind-bendingly empty that outer space itself looks like the California interstate at noon. Your brain deals with your feelings of helplessness by fantasizing that you're one of the lucky few who gets to witness the absolute end of the world.

This fantasy of doom is why people do a lot of the weird things they do . . . trek through deserts, build temples, start wars, vote Nader . . . all to get on the right side of the universe before they figure it's completely too late.

What was all that about, you ask?

You can't live like I do without wondering about fame from time to time.

Paris is famous exactly the way whoever invented the parking meter isn't.

It may be the Hilton family's money that allows us to live like we do, but it's her fame that really gets us around, gives us a place to be at any given moment, gives us a reason or at least an excuse to get on the plane. It is its own animal.

So, I've come to figure that's the real reason why Paris is famous, beyond her efforts to get noticed or her looks or connections . . . Paris Hilton is one of those things, one of those glimpses into the universe that twist people's minds like a Rubik's Cube in the hands of a nervous gorilla.

I think it goes like this: a normal person with a normal job goes on their lunch break at their job, sees Paris Hilton's image absolutely everywhere, asks a fan of hers what she does exactly, and either can't get a straight answer, or gets a stream of very enthusiastic "Nothing. She doesn't do anything" from the fan.

"Well, then why do you like her?" the person is forced to ask. "Can you explain it to me a little? Is it her charisma? Sure, she's pretty, but not overwhelmingly so. Lots of pretty people around. Why do you like her?"

The person then sees the Paris fan's face go blank like they've just been asked to sort out how many theoretical penguins you can fit on the head of a nonexistent pin, without any paper to scribble things on.

Looking into the blank face of the fan who loves without knowing why, our person wonders about that report they're supposed to have finished by the end of the day, a report that our person knows will serve no purpose but as one more bureaucratic cog in some imaginary machine, useless and unseen to all, which exists only to inadvertently get them fed for one more week.

Then the person looks at the image of Paris herself—a perfect blankness that

radiates out and completes the circuit with the blank face of the fan, forming a thing rarely seen in nature: a perfect vacuum.

Our person looking in at this Fan/Paris relationship has one horrifying, brain-meltingly incomprehensible glimpse into the very nature of the universe:

The universe is unfair.

It's so unfair that the word "unfair" fails its basic lack of fairness like the word "agony" fails the Ice Capades.

MAY 10 | 04 THE END

Well, it's about a year from when I started, and I've been asked to update things for the book release.

We did another *Simple Life*, billed as a cross-country trek but seemed like it was filmed in some warehouse in the middle of Mexico. Since the first program was so successful, the studio really lashed out with some cash and promised the CGI would be such that the show would look real this time . . . not, they muttered under their respective breaths, that it had to. Also they got us a real horse that turns out really doesn't react well to being spritzed with Binaca, even if its breath does smell "totally like a dead skunk's asshole, omigod."

By the time you read this, the new show will have aired, and you'll all be just a little bit sicker of what I have come to understand as my daily life.

You'll watch it, and then you'll likely complain that Paris is vapid, spoiled, clueless, and "what the hell does she have a television show for anyway, my uncle Dave is a billion times funnier and he has to milk bats for a living."

Don't bother—we know, and we don't care.

Well, half of that is true.

We don't know.

I introduced myself in this book by posing a question I didn't have an answer to . . . and nothing has changed. I still don't know why you pay attention to us and not that guy feverishly trying to create a pollution-free fuel out of sea water, or those people who spend all their days trying to cure cancer with dead monkey scrotums or whatever it is they do in those research facilities.

Maybe you see something in Paris that you wish you had; maybe you simply wish you were that something inside Paris. Either way, she has effectively become the icon she set out to be in a pretty short amount of time.

Think about it—she's famous for being famous . . . a real-life version of that M. C. Escher drawing where the hands reach out of the paper and make themselves be.

Can I explain that?

No.

I'm a small, badly dressed Chihuahua, not a philosopher.

I'll just pass along this thing I heard the Dalai Lama mumble to himself that one time as he walked by on the airplane:

"A shoe without a foot in it is still a shoe. A sock without a foot in it is merely laundry."

I can't do any better than that.

How else can you answer an unanswerable question, but with a koan.

I won't tell you that my owner is misunderstood, I'll tell you that she's about as understood as she needs to be to get to the next misunderstanding.

Well, that's what I got.

That, and a small closet full of angora sweaters.

I look like one of Flavor Flav's boogers most of the time, but I could do worse; I'm very well looked after—a mere bitch hasn't had a ride this good since Marie Antoinette before the butler let the mob in—and the ride is pretty interesting.

My name is Tink Hilton; I'm signing off now.

Five Things You Could Do to Improve Yourself

A List, in reverse order of "you know it's true, girlfriend":

5. Look at me. Now look at you. Look at me. Now look at you. Clear?

4. Start every morning with this question: "What else could I do for Paris Hilton?"

3. Why are you even talking to me? Who let you in here?

2. Are you tan? Couldn't you be tanner?

1. Let's stop lording that literacy thing over everybody. You don't have a sex life like the rest of us do, we get it already.